Brock University

Published in 2009 by
Binea Press, Inc.
512-1673 Richmond Street
London, Ontario, Canada N6G 2N3

Tel: 519.660.6424
Fax: 519.660.4449

E-mail: bineapress@bellnet.ca
www.bineapress.com

Distributed by:

Binea Press Inc.
519.660.6424

Library and Archives Canada Cataloguing in Publication

Bain, Richard (Richard G.), 1954-

Brock University / Richard Bain

Foreword by Ned Goodman

ISBN 978-0-978-3012-9-3

1. Brock University - Pictorial works. I. Title.

LE3.B93B35 2009   378.713'38   C2009-902178-1

Design by Pazzo Creative
London, Ontario, Canada
Tel: 519.660.6424

Printed in Canada by Friesens Corporation
Altona, Manitoba

Brock University

RICHARD BAIN

FOREWORD BY

NED GOODMAN

With gratitude to

The Walker Family and Walker Industries Holdings Limited

FOREWORD

From the moment I first set foot on the campus of Brock University, I knew I'd come to a place that was out of the ordinary. Aside from the natural beauty of the campus, I was, and continue to be, struck by the pervasive and genuine friendliness of students, faculty and staff at this mid-sized Ontario university. I've come to expect and appreciate that this richness and generosity of spirit is an integral part of the Brock experience, where there are daily demonstrations of people caring about people, both on campus and spilling into the broader community.

As Chancellor, I've had but a brief association with Brock University. However, it's been a meaningful and warm relationship. Nothing gives me greater pleasure in my role as Chancellor than to confer degrees at Brock's Convocation ceremonies. Fresh-thinking graduates, brimming with confidence and talent, step off Convocation stage and into a world where they'll be the social, cultural and economic leaders of the communities in which they settle. I've no doubt that they will continue to make a profound difference in this world.

I say continue to make, because many, if not most, of Brock's graduates have made positive contributions to their communities long before they receive their degrees. This is because, as part of its culture, Brock offers students, faculty and staff exceptional opportunities to develop both personally and academically.

The "both sides of the brain" experience can be seen in professors who turn mathematical equations into internationally renowned art, research opportunities made available to undergraduate students, or philanthropists whose passions span from corporate law to architecture and sculpture.

Brock's also about embracing a zest for life. Anyone who has attended a Brock Badgers game or competition will be impressed by the fervor and loyalty of the fans. And there's a reason for that. With dozens of national and provincial titles and the bragging rights to several Olympic medals, Brock has distinguished itself on the court, ice rink, field, track, pool, watercourse and floor.

The iconic Arthur Schmon Tower rises in the background, partly obscured by a blaze of colour on one of the trees in Jubilee Court.

Students study in the Plaza Building long after the sun has gone down.

But let's go back to those Convocation celebrations. In my role
as Chancellor, I also have the honour of meeting proud families
and friends of the graduates; unlike other universities, Brock
doesn't limit the number of people who want to share in this
joyful rite of passage. Families, many of whom helped to finance
their children's education, also helped to build and continue
to sustain this University, and we acknowledge with gratitude
their many contributions.

Indeed, if it weren't for Niagara families, this campus may
not even exist. By the late 1950s and early '60s, more and more
people were supporting the idea of a Niagara-based university
so that young people could receive a solid post-secondary
education without having to leave the area.

This sentiment gained traction in November 1957 when the
Allanburg Women's Institute presented a resolution asking the
Province of Ontario to "favourably consider the placing of a
university in the Niagara Peninsula."

By the autumn of 1962, the Brock Founders Committee was
incorporated. Committee members received approval for the
University, they developed an administrative and academic
plan and they began raising money. In a remarkable grassroots
effort, donations were made – $50 here, $100 there, $10
somewhere else – farmstead by farmstead, shop floor by
shop floor, community elder by community elder.

And in 1964, the effort paid off – Brock held its first
classes in the basement of the former St. Paul Street
United Church in St. Catharines.

What a tremendous distance Brock has travelled in almost 50 years! No longer is it a post-secondary institution known only for its undergraduate programs. As Chancellor, I've conferred, and expect to continue to confer, many master's and doctoral degrees upon outstanding graduate students from an impressive diversity of programs, individuals who understand that they are works in progress, that they'll learn by making mistakes, and that the dual qualities of humour and humility are an important part of lives well lived.

In terms of research, our facilities and programs are second to none. Brock's unafraid to take intellectual risks and develop new areas of knowledge, much of it at the intersection of disciplines. Academic programs are rigorous and experiential. A degree from Brock has value, exceptional value.

And it will only get better. In 2009, Brock launched a massive $75-million fundraising campaign to create much-needed space, bolster its research capacity and help generate new industries for Ontario's recession-racked economy. The Campaign, the largest in the University's history, is seeking funding for six major building initiatives, enhancing the student learning experience, and empowering teachers, researchers and innovators through library improvements and endowed research chairs.

But Brock's about more than brains. It's also about beauty. Brock is part of a protected UNESCO Biosphere Reserve. Its open space and trail systems are amenities used by the University community and Niagara residents. The campus is surrounded by some of the finest viticultural and fruit-growing farmland in the world, and the region's popular wine festivals draw thousands of tourists to Niagara each year. On a clear day, the mist from one of the world's most spectacular attractions, Niagara Falls, can be seen from the top floor of the Arthur Schmon Tower, the heart of the campus. Look in another direction, and Toronto's impressive skyline is visible across Lake Ontario.

Inviting and charming pockets of blossoming trees and water features, juxtaposed with the University's architecturally bold and dramatic buildings, provide a dynamic tension between natural and human achievements. During the summer, a farmers' market featuring local produce lures the Brock family to picnic tables set up in Jubilee Court. Hundreds of elementary and high school students, participating in a diversity of special interest camps,

BROCK IS PART OF A UNESCO BIOSPHERE RESERVE; LUSH VEGETATION
TUMBLES OVER ANCIENT ROCK ON THE BRUCE TRAIL.

A SUNNY DAY DRAWS STUDENTS OUTSIDE AS THEY WALK TO THEIR CLASSES.

boisterously gather in Walker Court at noon where a waterfall tumbles over well-placed boulders. Naturalized and manicured grounds co-exist, delighting the senses.

Finally, it would be remiss of me indeed not to mention Brock's namesake, Maj.-Gen. Sir Isaac Brock. The brilliant military strategist, killed by a musket ball in Niagara during the War of 1812, would have been astounded to know that two centuries later, a university in Niagara would bear his name. And he'd doubtless be pleased to know that Alphie's, still one of the most intimate and beautiful gathering places on campus, is named after his beloved horse.

In the last few years, the University has remembered the death of Sir Isaac in a solemn flag-lowering ceremony, complete with historical re-enactors in period costume and a multi-gun salute. "Surgite! Push on!" – considered to be the general's dying utterance – is the University motto.

It's this blend of fascinating past, dynamic present and bold future that makes Brock what it is. What it's not is a dusty, ivy-covered institution mired in old ways of thinking. Brock's strength comes from the optimistic passion of its people – students, faculty and staff who are forward thinking, community minded and motivated.

I've come to admire Brock on many different levels, and I'm proud to be the Chancellor of a university that boldly dares to be out of the ordinary.

Ned Goodman

UPPER: MEMBERS OF THE STUDENT WELCOMING AWARENESS TEAM DO SOME HEAVY LIFTING
AS THEY HELP STUDENTS MOVE INTO RESIDENCE DURING ORIENTATION WEEK.

LOWER: PARENTS SPEND SOME QUIET TIME WITH THEIR DAUGHTER DURING
RESIDENCE MOVE-IN DAY AS SHE STARTS AN EXCITING NEW CHAPTER IN HER LIFE.

JODY THOMAS, FORMER PRESIDENT OF THE BROCK UNIVERSITY STUDENTS' UNION, CAN'T CONTAIN HIS EXCITEMENT DURING RESIDENCE MOVE-IN DAY.

FRIENDS IN RESIDENCE TAKE TIME OUT TO CHAT ABOUT THEIR DAY.

You are here: daughter and mother find their way around campus during Orientation Week.

Making candy floss, being dunked in the tank and racing
through an air castle are some of the fun-filled activities
that entertain students during Orientation Week.

Brock University has made a huge difference
in my life. After working for the local newspaper
for 12 years, I found that I could no longer
do my job, due to the progressive nature of my
inherited neuromuscular disease. My mother,
in her wisdom, suggested I return to school.
I began Brock as a mature student with my
goal on a major in death and dying and
graduated after finishing a paper on sex and
disability! Brock gave me the education and the
confidence to begin an organization that helped
thousands of people worldwide with my disease.
Now in my 60s, I'm still writing, painting and
hosting websites that help people with disabilities
travel and find resources to make their lives easier.
I feel blessed that Brock exists in our community.

Linda Crabtree
BA, Psychology, '87
Honorary doctorate, '94

TUCKED AWAY IN THE MACKENZIE CHOWN
COMPLEX, THE SPECTACULAR POND INLET
IS A NATURAL GATHERING SPOT FOR
STUDENTS, STAFF AND FACULTY.

ABOVE: FRESH PRODUCE FROM LOCAL GROWERS ENTICES THE LUNCHTIME
CROWD TO THE WEEKLY SUMMER MARKET IN JUBILEE COURT.

RIGHT: STUDENTS TAKE A BREAK FROM THEIR STUDIES.

ABOVE: WAR OF 1812 RE-ENACTORS GREET GUESTS
TO GENERAL BROCK'S OCTOBER SOIREE.

RIGHT: HORSE-DRAWN CARRIAGES DELIVER GUESTS
TO GENERAL BROCK'S OCTOBER SOIREE AT
QUEEN'S LANDING IN NIAGARA-ON-THE-LAKE.

ABOVE: TABLEAUX VIVANTS FROM THE MARILYN I. WALKER
SCHOOL OF FINE AND PERFORMING ARTS.

LEFT: DRAMATIC ARTS STUDENTS ENROLLED IN THE
MARILYN I. WALKER SCHOOL OF FINE AND PERFORMING ARTS
ENTERTAIN GUESTS AT THE FIRST ANNUAL GENERAL BROCK'S
OCTOBER SOIREE. SEATED TO THE RIGHT IN THE SCARLET JACKET
IS ACTOR GUY BANNERMAN PORTRAYING SIR ISAAC BROCK.

WOODEN RAMPS LEAD TO THE SECLUDED ALPHIE'S
RESTAURANT, A FAVOURITE DINING SPOT ON CAMPUS
FOR FACULTY, STAFF AND GRADUATE STUDENTS.

ABOVE: Unable to resist a beautiful day,
two students take their studies outside.

RIGHT: Professor Martin Head, right, leads
students to a rocky outcrop on Brock's campus.

When I graduated from Brock in the early
'70s, I vowed to return one day as a faculty
member. My experience as an undergraduate
student proved to me that Brock is a university
where students are encouraged to engage in learning
with a passion, where the boundaries of academia
are expanded into action-research that has the
potential of changing the world in which we live.
When I returned to Brock as a professor, I retained
this experience as my philosophy of teaching.

Dorothy Griffiths
Associate Dean
Faculty of Social Sciences

ALL TOGETHER NOW: THERE'S A
BLUR OF ACTIVITY AS DRAMATIC ARTS
STUDENTS PERFORM AN ACTIVITY
CALLED "VIEWPOINTS."

DRAMATIC ARTS STUDENTS PERFORM IN "SMASH!", ONE OF TWO MAINSTAGE
PRODUCTIONS THAT STUDENTS MOUNT IN THE SEAN O'SULLIVAN THEATRE,
A 500-SEAT FACILITY WITH A THRUST STAGE.

UPPER: AN ELABORATE COSTUME IS FITTED BY THE WARDROBE
CO-ORDINATOR IN THE WARDROBE DESIGN SHOP.

LOWER: SECOND-YEAR DRAMATIC ARTS STUDENTS ARE ENROLLED IN THE CLOWNING
COURSE THAT INCLUDES PERSONAL CLOWN, MASK, MOVEMENT, AND SCENE STUDIES
EXPLORING ENSEMBLE AND INDIVIDUAL PERFORMANCE.

ABOVE: SWEATIN' IN THE ZONE: BROCK HAS ONE OF THE FINEST FITNESS FACILITIES IN NIAGARA.

RIGHT: THE SUSPENDED RUNNING TRACK IN THE WALKER COMPLEX IS AN EXTREMELY WELL-USED FACILITY AND OFFERS A GREAT VIEW OF CAMPUS.

My music has taken me around the world, but my home and heart are still here in St. Catharines. One of the jewels in our region's crown is Brock University, which recognized me with an honorary doctorate degree in 1995. It is with great pride that I now serve as an ambassador representing this University.

Walter Ostanek
Grammy Award winner
Honorary doctorate, 1995

ABOVE: STUDENTS IN A LIFE DRAWING CLASS ARE INSPIRED BY A MODEL IN THE BACKGROUND.

RIGHT: A VISUAL ARTS STUDENT ADDS ANOTHER BRUSH STROKE TO HER CANVAS IN THE STUDIO.

ABOVE: WINE TASTING TAKES PLACE IN A WINE
SENSORY LAB UNDER CONTROLLED RED LIGHTING.

LEFT: THE FAIRMONT HOTELS AND RESORTS WINE
CELLAR, ONE OF THE LARGEST IN CANADA WITH A
43,000-BOTTLE CAPACITY, IS LOCATED IN THE COOL
CLIMATE OENOLOGY AND VITICULTURE INSTITUTE, AN
INTERNATIONALLY RECOGNIZED FACILITY FOR THE STUDY
OF GRAPE GROWING AND WINE MAKING.

INNISKILLIN HALL, HOME TO THE INTERNATIONALLY RECOGNIZED COOL
CLIMATE OENOLOGY AND VITICULTURE INSTITUTE, OPENED IN 1999.

A PERFECT AUTUMN DAY.

Long ago, in the Age before Middle Girth, there was the Tower — and only the Tower.
The pub came later — to great acclaim. There was smoking in the library stairwell;
squatters in the study carrels; coffee in the basement cafeteria; and that unfortunate week when
we watched the first Canada-Soviet hockey series instead of doing our seminar readings ...

Peter Goodspeed
Foreign affairs writer, National Post
BA, Politics, '73

A COLD BEER AT ISAAC'S — AN INTEGRAL PART OF THE BROCK STUDENT EXPERIENCE.

A COZY GATHERING PLACE AT THE THE DAILY GRIND ABOVE ISAAC'S.

Brock has changed a great deal over the years. There are the big differences, such as new buildings for teaching, learning and research. There are new student-centred facilities like the Matheson Learning Commons — it is a tremendous honour that this welcoming space bears my name. There is the rapidly growing number of undergraduate and graduate degree programs in a huge diversity of fields. There are also other significant changes, especially in technology. Gone are the punch cards and slide rules I recall from Brock's early days. An entire information technology department now provides a broad range of cutting-edge services to the Brock family. How times have changed!

Bill Matheson
Professor Emeritus
Political Science

SCOTIABANK HALL INCLUDES THE COMPUTER COMMONS, LEFT, THE LARGEST COMPUTER FACILITY FOR STUDENT USE ON CAMPUS.

ABOVE: THE WALKER COMPLEX IS A DRAMATIC BACKDROP FOR
THE LANDSCAPE OF TALL ORNAMENTAL GRASSES.

LEFT: A HUGE EXPANSE OF GLASS IS LOCATED AT THE END OF THE IAN D. BEDDIS GYMNASIUM.

From the Schmon Tower to Alphie's Trough to the bleachers
that were invaded by the 'bucketheads' game after game
— my four years that were spent in the incredible world that
is Brock University will never be forgotten ... I will always be
very proud to hang my degree high and call myself a Badger!

Rick Campanelli
Co-host, Entertainment Tonight Canada
BA, Physical Education, '94

ABOVE: SMILING BROCK STUDENTS ATTEND THE PEN CENTRE
GRANDE PARADE DURING THE NIAGARA WINE FESTIVAL.

RIGHT: ALL HAIL BOOMER THE BADGER! THE UNIVERSITY
MASCOT TAKES CENTRE STAGE ON THE BROCK FLOAT IN THE
PEN CENTRE GRANDE PARADE IN DOWNTOWN ST. CATHARINES.

UPPER: A FUTURE BROCK STUDENT HAS HER FACE PAINTED BY A CURRENT STUDENT
AT THE NIAGARA WINE FESTIVAL IN DOWNTOWN ST. CATHARINES.

LOWER: FRIENDSHIPS ARE REKINDLED DURING BROCK DAYS AND ALUMNI HOMECOMING
AT THE NIAGARA WINE FESTIVAL IN DOWNTOWN ST. CATHARINES.

UPPER: COLOUR ME PURPLE: STUDENTS COLLAPSE IN HAPPY EXHAUSTION
AFTER THE CELEBRATED ANNUAL GRAPE STOMP ON CAMPUS.

LOWER: SLUICING THE JUICE: STOMPERS ARE HOSED DOWN AFTER THE GRAPE CRUSH.

I am proud to be a Brock alumna and
I am particularly proud to be a graduate
of the first Co-op Accounting class. To celebrate
the 25th anniversary of the program
in 2005, my good friend Lyman Gardiner
and I spearheaded a fundraising initiative
with our former classmates, resulting in the
largest class gift in Brock's history. I encourage
you to step up when your calling comes.

Debi Rosati
Corporate director, RosatiNet Inc.
BAdmin, '84

A LIGHT MIST SHROUDS THE PLAZA
BUILDING, ONE OF THE NEWER
BUILDINGS ON THE BROCK CAMPUS.

UPPER: PHYSICAL EDUCATION STUDENTS SPELL OUT THE
NAME OF THEIR ALMA MATER IN THE BOB DAVIS GYM.

LOWER: FINDING BALANCE: TWO STUDENTS PERFORM A
ROUTINE ON THE BALANCE BEAM IN ONE OF BROCK'S GYMS.

LEFT: A STUDENT CATCHES UP ON THE NEWS IN THE WALKER COMPLEX.

Brock lacrosse players, top, and soccer
players, below, watch the action on the field.

A soccer match at Brock's athletic playing field.

GIVE ME A B! BROCK CHEERLEADERS SHOW THEIR BEST STUFF
IN THE PEN CENTRE GRANDE PARADE, ONE OF THE SIGNATURE
EVENTS OF THE ANNUAL NIAGARA WINE FESTIVAL.

A Brock rugby player breaks away from opposing players.

FORMER COACH CHRIS CRITELLI GOES OVER GAME
STRATEGIES WITH THE WOMEN'S BASKETBALL TEAM.

STRETCHING TO THE HOOP: BROCK WOMEN'S BASKETBALL
TEAM TAKES ON OPPONENTS AT A HOME GAME. GO BADGERS!

When I came to Brock, I had little idea
of what I wanted to do with my life,
but I'm leaving with a clear direction and
promising job prospects. It's hard to say
whether the textbooks, journal articles and
long papers will stay in my mind, but I do
know for certain that my Brock experience
will always be a part of who I am. I will
forever remember my first day of residence,
terrified to leave home, and my last day in
residence, sharing hugs and tears with friends
as we said our goodbyes. Brock Days, the Niagara
Wine Festival and other activities make me proud
of the ways that Brock and the community work
together to help the community become stronger.
The friends I've made here at Brock are reasons
to think fondly of this school. Brock has made
me who I am, and as I move on, I find myself
proudly reflecting on the positive impact that
this University has had on my life.

Meaghan Moore
BA, Communications Studies, '09

NIAGARA HAS ESTABLISHED ITSELF AS ONE
OF THE WORLD'S PREMIER ROWING CENTRES.
BROCK ROWERS HEAD TO THE WATER
FOR AN EARLY-MORNING PRACTICE.

Autumn sunshine lights up brilliantly coloured
foliage on the trees in Jubilee Court.

WITH BACKPACK AND HELMET IN PLACE, A CYCLIST LEAVES CAMPUS.

The beauty of Pond Inlet.

It is difficult to imagine a Niagara without Brock University. The institution is woven into the economic and social fabric of our community. Niagara Region is proud to be a strong supporter of Brock — a vital community partner and resource — as it works to produce the leaders who will shape and contribute to Niagara's future growth and prosperity.

Peter Partington
Chair, Regional Municipality of Niagara

Students perch on comfortable stools in the Matheson Learning Commons.

A WINTRY WALK TO CLASS.

Bundled up against a Canadian winter.

Drifting and falling snow accompany a student walking near the Decew Residence for students.

It is a great pleasure and privilege to be free to think about the mysteries of life at the molecular level. This was made possible by living in a wealthy, open, respectful and nurturing nation that is Canada. My family immigrated to this country in 1957, where I was able to take advantage of excellent educational opportunities and to use all of the necessary resources that have entirely fulfilled my greatest academic and research aspirations. Freedom is synonymous with the fulfilment of science as is literature, art and most other creative human activities.

Vincenzo De Luca
Tier 1 Canada Research Chair
Faculty of Mathematics and Science

SENIOR DEMONSTRATOR SERGIO PAONE
FROM THE DEPARTMENT OF CHEMISTRY
HOLDS THINGS STEADY DURING A
DEMONSTRATION IN ONE OF BROCK'S LABS.

CUTTING-EDGE RESEARCH TAKES PLACE IN A CAMPUS BIOLOGY LAB.

A RESEARCHER IN PLANT BIOTECHNOLOGY WORKS OUT OF THE LAB OF
PROFESSOR VINCENZO DE LUCA, WHO CREATES SPECIALIZED PLANT CELL
FACTORIES USING THE PROCESS OF RATIONAL METABOLIC ENGINEERING.

I've enjoyed a long and warm relationship with Brock University. My family roots run deep in Niagara, and it was with great excitement when I and other Niagarans watched the Arthur Schmon Tower rise storey by storey on the crest of the Niagara Escarpment back in the '60s. I believe intensely in Brock's bold vision and I'm proud of the leadership role the University continues to play in the economic, cultural and social future of our region and beyond.

David S. Howes
Chair, Brock Board of Trustees

CANADIAN TIRE BRIDGE CONNECTS THE
ALUMNI STUDENT CENTRE WITH TARO HALL.

Athletes work out in the eight-person rowing tank at the Leo LeBlanc Rowing Centre, which opened in 1995 and is the only facility of its kind at a Canadian university. The facility also includes 13 rowing ergometers and a weight-lifting room for winter training as well as secondary workouts during on-water season. Brock Rowing often works with Rowing Canada and Row Ontario to host winter training and identification camps for national and provincial teams.

Members of the women's swim team power through
the water at Brock's Olympic-sized pool.

UPPER: BROCK BUSINESS STUDENTS COMPARE NOTES.

LOWER: BROCK'S WIRELESS TECHNOLOGY ACCOMMODATES STUDENTS IN THE
MATHESON LEARNING COMMONS AS THEY WORK ON THEIR LAPTOP COMPUTERS.

RIGHT: AN EXPANSIVE HALLWAY IN ACADEMIC SOUTH.

ABOVE: A SNOW-CAPPED BUST OF ROBERT WELCH, BROCK'S FIFTH CHANCELLOR.

RIGHT: A HEAVY SNOWFALL TRANSFORMS THE CAMPUS INTO A WINTER WONDERLAND.

Brock University has a dynamic academic culture that strongly supports my interdisciplinary work in mathematics and art. As a teacher, it's satisfying and exciting to be part of our internationally renowned Mathematics Integrated with Computing and Applications program, where students use computers to create interactive explorations of mathematics. As an artist, I hope that my work will connect people emotionally to the remarkable complexity and unity that is inherent within the rich mathematical objects that inspire my images. Outside of the classroom, my walks in the beautiful woods around Brock's campus have sparked some of the ideas for my artwork and research.

Bill Ralph
Associate Professor
Faculty of Mathematics and Science

MATHEMATICS PROFESSOR BILL RALPH
PEEKS OUT FROM BEHIND ONE OF HIS
INTERNATIONALLY ACCLAIMED
PIECES OF ARTWORK.

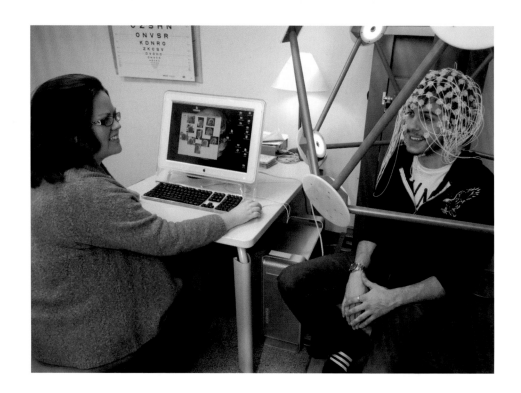

UPPER: PHD CANDIDATE MALINDA DESJARLAIS TRACKS THE EYE
MOVEMENT OF A PARTICIPANT SURFING THE INTERNET.

LOWER: RESEARCH ASSISTANT ALLISON FLYNN TESTS BRAIN ACTIVITY
PATTERNS IN PSYCHOLOGY UNDERGRADUATE STEFON VAN NOORDT.

UPPER: GRADUATE STUDENT DAN HARRISS TRAINS ON A STATE-OF-THE-ART SKATING TREADMILL
USED TO RESEARCH BEST PRACTICES IN SKATING MECHANICS AND HOCKEY DEVELOPMENT.
PROFESSOR KELLY LOCKWOOD PIONEERED AND IS THE LEAD SCIENTIST OF THE LAB.

LOWER: MARNIE LAMBERT, A GRADUATE OF BROCK'S EDUCATION PROGRAM,
TEACHES A CLASS OF EAGER YOUNG STUDENTS AT SMITH SCHOOL IN GRIMSBY.

Hitting the right notes: students practise in the
music rehearsal labs in the Arthur Schmon Tower.

GEOGRAPHY STUDENTS WORK ON A CARTOGRAPHY ASSIGNMENT IN THE UNIVERSITY MAP LIBRARY.

above: Spring blossoms by the Mackenzie Chown Complex,
named after a former mayor of St. Catharines.

left: Pond Inlet, a favourite spot on campus.

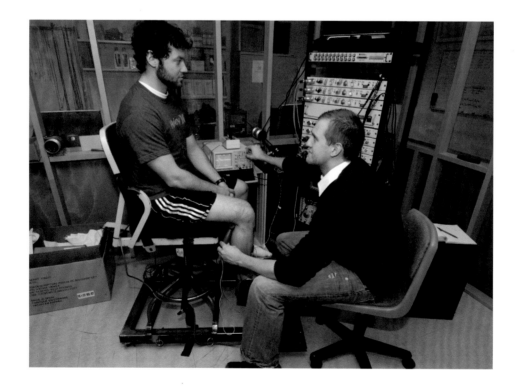

upper: Students Kelsey Van Den Heede, left, and Caitlin Cushbec compare notes in a Faculty of Applied Health Sciences anatomy lab.

lower: Graduate student Kyle McIntosh, seated, collects data for his thesis from another student in an electromyographic kinesiology lab.

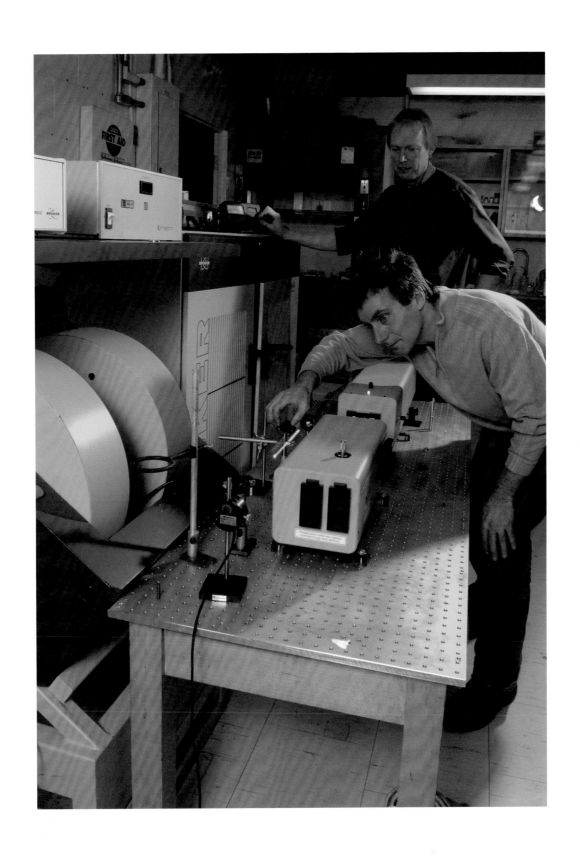

PROFESSORS DOUG BRUCE, FOREGROUND, AND
ART VAN DER EST WORK WITH LASERS IN ONE OF BROCK'S SCIENCE LABS.

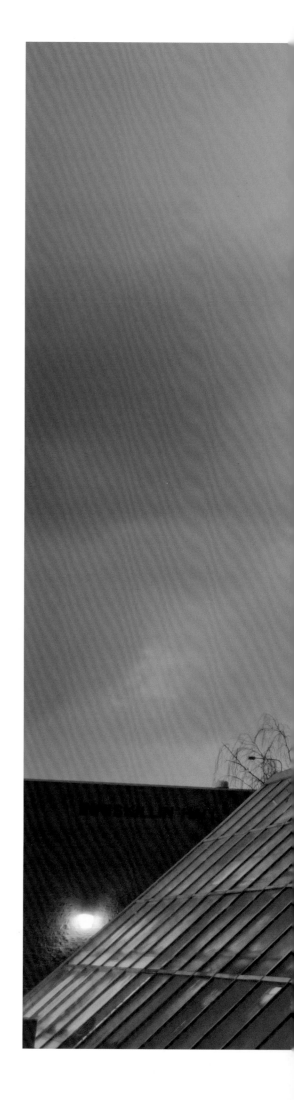

ABOVE: STUDENTS WRITE EXAMS AT DUSK.

RIGHT: THE ALAN EARP RESIDENCE, NAMED AFTER
THE SECOND PRESIDENT AND VICE-CHANCELLOR OF THE
UNIVERSITY, LOOMS BEHIND THE ALUMNI GREENHOUSE.

*I thoroughly enjoyed my time at Brock.
The education I received solidified my
interest in serving our community through
politics. I could not have received better training
anywhere, or gained a better understanding
of the importance of clear and effective
communications. I am very proud to call myself
an alumnus and I am delighted to see how
Brock is continuing to grow and evolve,
particularly in research and development.*

Rick Dykstra
St. Catharines Member of Parliament
BA, Political Science, '97

SHHHHHH! STUDENTS CONCENTRATE ON
THEIR EXAMS IN THE IAN D. BEDDIS GYM.

A DELIGHTED STUDENT CLUTCHES HIS DEGREE
AND CALLS FRIENDS WITH THE GOOD NEWS.

THE STERLING SILVER MACE IS AN IMPORTANT PART OF BROCK'S CONVOCATION CEREMONIES. IT WAS PRESENTED AS A GIFT FROM THE PEOPLE OF THE BAILIWICK OF GUERNSEY, BIRTHPLACE OF MAJ.-GEN. SIR ISAAC BROCK, IN 1992.

ABOVE: SHARING THE JOY OF ACHIEVEMENT.

LEFT: A PROUD FAMILY ON CONVOCATION DAY.

UPPER: HIGH FIVES AFTER CONVOCATION.

LOWER: THE BIG DAY CAPTURED ON CAMERA.

RIGHT: THE PATH OF POSSIBILITIES, A SCULPTURE BY ISRAELI ARTIST
ILAN AVERBUCH, RISES DRAMATICALLY ON CAMPUS GROUNDS.

Bright yellow umbrellas at the Walker Complex courtyard
are reflected in the water and in the windows.

Windows reflect Pond Inlet.

A QUIET MOMENT DURING A NATURE WALK ON CAMPUS.

Canadian Tire Bridge connects Taro Hall with the Plaza
Building, Campus Store and Student Alumni Centre.

A SPRAY OF ORNAMENTAL GRASS ADDS TO THE ATTRACTIVE LANDSCAPE.

As the mayor of St. Catharines, I am proud
to have received my start in public office
as a representative on the Brock University
Students' Union. This experience ignited
in me a passion for public service that led me
to the office I now hold. I know my experience
at Brock University put me on the path to success.

Brian McMullan
Mayor of St. Catharines
BA, Political Science and History, '80

TARO HALL, WHICH CURRENTLY
HOUSES THE FACULTY OF BUSINESS.

Japanese flowering cherry trees, a gift donated to Brock by the Sakura Project in 2003, lose their leaves as winter approaches. The trees represent friendship and goodwill between Japan and Canada and mark the 75th anniversary of diplomatic relations between the two countries.

BARE BRANCHES AND A CARPET OF LEAVES IN JUBILEE COURT.

I'm proud to be a Silver Badger, a graduate of Brock's very first honours class. My years at Brock were special, and I immersed myself in the experience. It was a thrill to be president of the Brock University Students' Union in my graduating year — I knew almost everyone on campus because Brock was so small — and I've had a long association with the University ever since. I will always cherish those memories.

Ian D. Beddis
BSc, '68
Honorary doctorate, '00

THE STRIKING MACKENZIE CHOWN
COMPLEX WAS DESIGNED BY
INTERNATIONALLY RESPECTED
ARCHITECT RAYMOND MORIYAMA.

ACKNOWLEDGEMENTS

My experience at Brock was nothing short of incredible. The students, staff and faculty all share something in common – they truly care about learning and about each other. Perhaps it is the fact that this university, although it continues to grow, has retained a sense of community... a sense of intimacy. Or perhaps it is its unique location, perched atop the naturally beautiful Niagara Escarpment. As I wandered the campus for 10 months, this sense of community and helpfulness continued to impress me.

It was an honour to have Ned Goodman agree to write the foreword for this book. As Chancellor, he continues to witness first hand the Brock experience, and his writing reflects his passion for this university.

Invaluable to this project was the advice and guidance that I received from Martha Nelson, Dean Lorenz, Kevin Grout, Trudy Lockyer, Joan Wiley and Wendy Bakker. I would also like to thank Dr. Jack Lightstone, David Petis, Steven Pillar and Luaine Hathaway for their ongoing assistance.

Several individuals shared their memories and vision of Brock. My thanks go to Ian Beddis, Rick Campanelli, Linda Crabtree, Vincenzo De Luca, Rick Dykstra, Peter Goodspeed, Dorothy Griffiths, David Howes, Bill Matheson, Brian McMullan, Meaghan Moore, Walter Ostanek, Peter Partington, Bill Ralph and Debi Rosati.

Too numerous to mention were the countless staff, administration, faculty and students who went out of their way to accommodate requests for photography. This book would not have been possible without their help. Also, special thanks to the design team at Pazzo Creative for their incredible talent at taking a group of photographic images and text, and producing a finished work. Thanks also to Tom Klassen and Elvira Filion from Friesens Book Division for co-ordinating the production and printing of this book.

I extend my heartfelt thanks to my wife, Joan, who continually encourages me to stick to my passions. Whenever I return from assignment, she is eager to see the images I have captured and to hear the stories associated with each one. Thanks also to my children, Caroline, Daniel, Brett and Jordan, who are always interested in my projects, and who, with my wife, accompany me when their busy schedules permit.

I hope that this book keeps the memory alive for those of you who are fortunate enough to have an affiliation with this great university. I am envious of those who have had the opportunity to spend more than the 10 months that I did on this truly beautiful campus. This is a university filled with history, academic excellence, spirit and beauty. I hope all who take the time to visit this campus once more, through these images and writings, remember how fortunate we all are for the gifts that Brock continues to give to the community and the world.

Richard Bain